# The
# Three
# Primary
# Resources

Getting from here to more

Ashton Fourie

**Other books by Ashton**
*When you lose yourself ... do you know where to go looking for you?*
*Real Dreams*
*Developing the Heart of a Leader*

# Contents

# Start Here

If you are reading this book, chances are that you are reading it in the hope to learn how to get to more.

More for some people would be more happiness, or more freedom. For others, it would be about being more effective, or having more impact on their environment. You might be reading this because you are a leader, and you want your organisation to achieve more.

The philosophy of the Three Primary Resources does not prescribe what you have to call success – but it does give you a structure to help you to think about growing that success in a balanced way

It doesn't matter where your life is at, at the moment. By using the philosophy of the Three Primary Resources, you can begin to evaluate your life as it is now, and begin to make better decisions that can help you consistently and systematically improve your life.

You are here. Start here.

# We All Have Them

This book is about Three Primary Resources, and two basic tools that can be used to systematically increase the availability of those Three Resources in your life.

Each of us in modern society needs these Three Primary Resources. And every one of us has to a greater or lesser extent, access to these Three Primary Resources.

- One of these Resources is given in exact equal measure to every person every day – and yet we don't all seem to ever have the same amount.
- One of them every person has, but in different measures – and we can influence on how much of it we have access to.
- And one of them we have to make – and the more of it we make, the more of it we seem to get access to.

We all also have the tools needed to increase our access to these Three Primary Resources in our lives.

Why do we call these Primary Resources?

Resources are things that we use to achieve something in life. These three are called the Primary Resources, because anything you want to achieve in life requires you to apply these three resources.

So what are the Three Primary Resources?

# The Three Primary Resources

The Three Primary Resources are: Available Time, Energy, and Money.

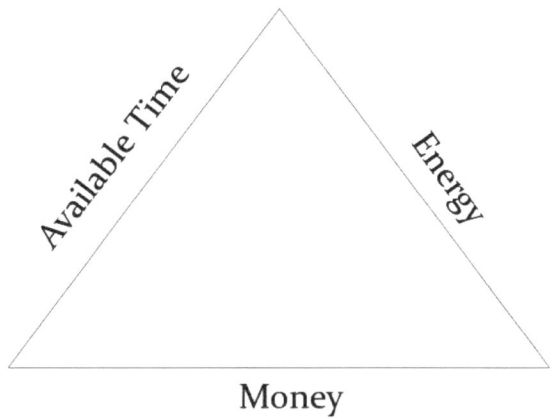

There may be some different interpretations of each of these, so let me take a moment to pause on the meaning of each of these Three Resources, in the context of this philosophy.

## Available Time

Available Time is time that you can apply to achieve the things that are important to you in life. I know one could try to convince yourself that you don't have to do anything, and therefore in theory we all have 24 hours available to us every day. But in reality many of us are caught in situations where we spend a lot of our time doing things we don't want to do, and we don't have a lot of choice over that.

There was a time in my life when I was working about 16 hours a day, seven days a week most weeks, and that barely earned me enough to make ends meet. The work I was doing wasn't achieving much of what was really important to me in life. The reality of that kind of situation, in which many people find themselves, is that Available Time is very limited.

For this reason, you must be very, very careful about the habits you acquire, and the commitments you make. Commitments and habits are two massive consumers of time. The moment you've committed yourself to doing something, you've given up some of your time. Make enough commitments, get involved in enough things, try to please enough other people, and you will find yourself impoverished of time. Similarly, once you've formed a habit, it eats your time, without question, every time you do it. For example a habit of sitting and "relaxing" in front of the TV for an hour after work, is a habit that will consume about 250 of your hours every year.

# Energy

Energy refers to physical energy as well as what could be called emotional, or motivational energy.

Sometimes it is easier to understand the meaning of energy when we think of what is a lack of energy.

Utter tiredness – when you cannot keep your eyes open, or physical exhaustion, when you can no longer lift a hand or foot – that would be the end of your physical energy.

Utter depression would be the end of your motivational and emotional energy. If you have no ability to motivate yourself to take any form of action, then you have run out of emotional and motivational energy.

Allowing yourself to reach a point of severe burnout is a way in which you can get yourself to reach the end of your energy. Sometimes anxiety, grief, and other powerfully painful emotions can drain our energy.

Illness, severe exertion, or sleep deprivation over a period of time can drain our physical energy.

Working on stuff that you don't enjoy, with people you don't like, and achieving goals that have no value for you, are some of the best ways to drain your energy.

# Money

For most of us, the definition of money can be simply exactly what most of us understand it to mean: The currency used to buy and sell things in your country, such as Dollars, Euros, Pounds, Rands, and so on.

But there may be situations where you need to allow yourself to take a somewhat broader, and more accurate view of money, as being a form of exchange. There are times in life, where direct access to money is a challenge, but through effective application of the other two resources, we can generate value, and convert that value into something that can result over time in obtaining decision making power over the application of money.

By thinking of money purely as a resource, rather than an end in itself, we also free ourselves from the need of ownership, and recognize that what we need, is access to the use of it. Resources are not in themselves valuable. Their value lie in their use, and this is particularly true of money. Ownership has its own benefits, such as autonomy to apply resources that you own in any way you want. But we must understand that the aim of life is not to own resources, but to apply resources effectively. And to apply them, you need to have at the very least access to them.

Mother Teresa is not known for her ownership of millions of dollars, but for her impact on millions of people. And a lot of that impact was achieved through people providing her and her organization with the resources needed to achieve their goals.

The purpose of money is to provide exchange. Generally, it is just easier to get what you want, if you can offer legal tender in the form of money, so you should generally aim to convert whatever value you are creating, into money, or some easily convertible form of asset if you want to be able to use the money.

I thought for a long time about whether I should not call this third resource "Capital," in order to include useful assets, such as cars, houses, buildings, machinery, factories, businesses and so on. But then I realized that even if you have these assets, and you have no money, you are still stuck. I have seen businesses with a strong balance sheet still take strain when they hit serious cash flow problems at inconvenient times.

So I decided to stick with money. You can use money to purchase and use these assets. But you cannot always quickly convert these assets back to money, if money is what you really need. You can always put money to the use you need it for, but you cannot always put these assets to the use you need it for.

With that I am not saying you should not purchase or lease capital assets in order to utilize them. By all means do. But don't do it to the point of finding yourself not having the money to do what needs to be done to maximize the value that you get from these assets.

# How Big Is Your Life?

When we think of these Three Primary Resources as the three sides of a triangle, the surface area of the triangle represents the "surface" of your life.

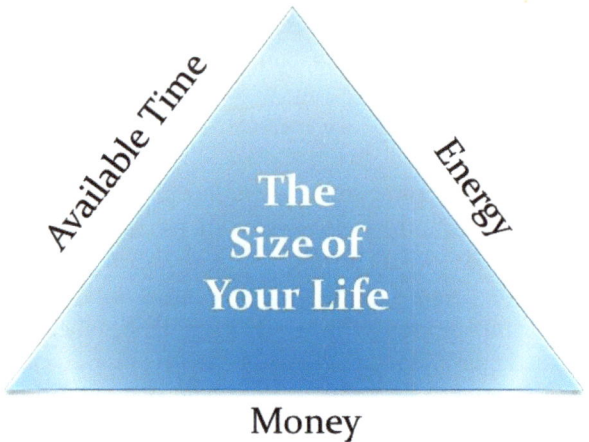

For different people, this surface can have different meanings. For many people it's about the impact that they can have. The bigger the surface, the bigger the impact you can have. For some people it's about their ability to live out their dreams. The bigger the surface, the bigger the dreams you will be able to successfully pursue. For others it's about lifestyle. The bigger your surface, the more expansive a lifestyle you can live.

If you want to make the surface bigger, you need to increase one, two, or three of these. The most effective way to increase the size of the surface is to increase the three of them in a balanced way. By striving to always keep the three sides the same length, you will be able to create the most systematic, balanced, and fulfilling increase in your life.

Each of us have at least two of these resources, and it is possible for you, right now, exactly where you are, to start growing your life from where it is, to where you want it to be. The trick is simply to take what you have, and begin to systematically increase it.

To increase these three, we need to use a basic set of tools – tools we have all been given as part of our package of being human...

# Tools for Increase

Each human being is given two simple tools that we can use to continually expand the size of our triangle: Creativity and Skills.

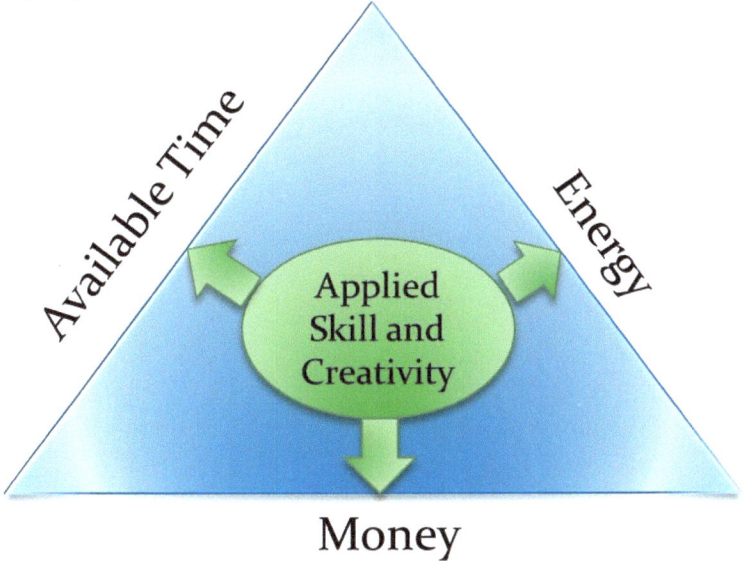

Applied Skill and Creativity

Available Time

Energy

Money

Skills are very simply the things you are able to do. It is generally made up of some knowledge, understanding, wisdom, and experience.

Creativity is your ability to come up with ideas.

Ideas alone, however, will not help you build much. It is only when you build the skill to enable you to put those ideas into forms that are useful to society, and figure out ways to make them available to society in such a way, that you get rewarded for that, that your ideas can help you build a bigger life.

Together, skill and creativity gives you the ability to combine resources in such a way that you can create increase.

For example if you have some time available, you have some money, and you have the motivational energy, you can use your skills and creativity to come up with a new business idea that can generate more money. You can use that money to employ professional managers, freeing up your time, and go on a great vacation, to boost your energy levels.

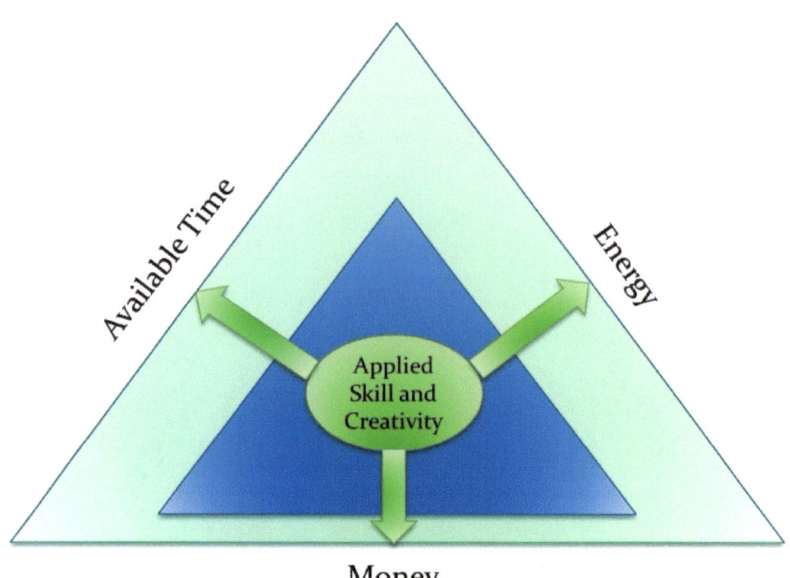

# If you have Two, You can make the Third

If you have enough of two of these, but lack one, you can use those two, and apply your skill and creativity to build the third one.

For example, let's say your energy levels are high, and you have enough money, but you lack time:

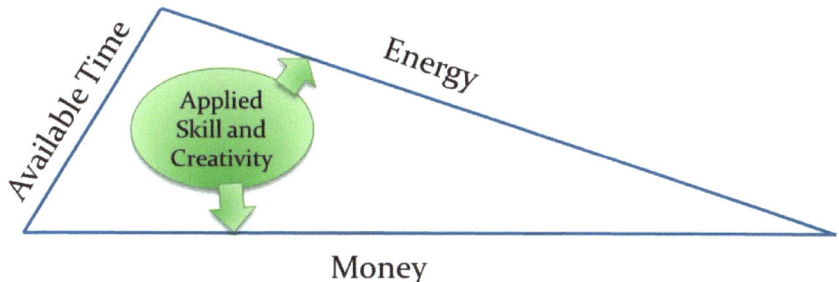

Then you can take your money and energy, use your skill and creativity to identify some areas of your life that you could get other people to help you with, design some clear requirements, and hire people or service companies to do some of the things that are keeping you busy.

This will use up some of your money and energy, but it will free up some of your time, and bring your triangle back into balance.

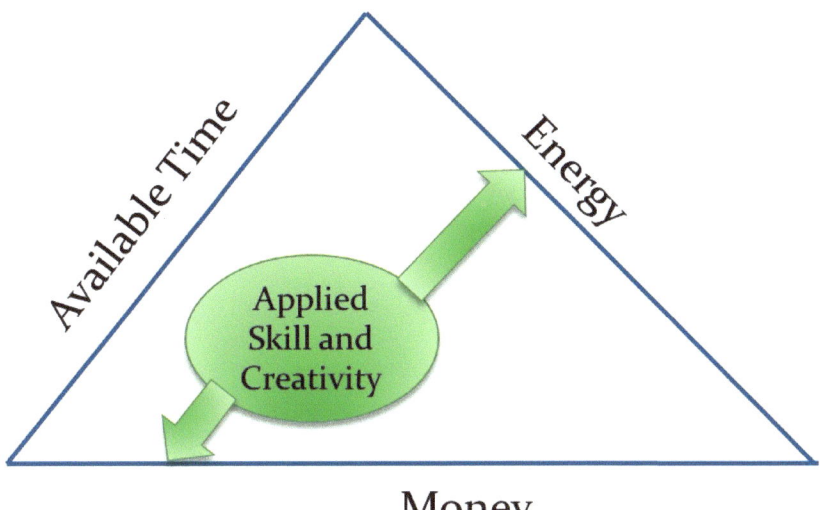

Similarly, if you have some time available, and you have enough money, but you are low on energy:

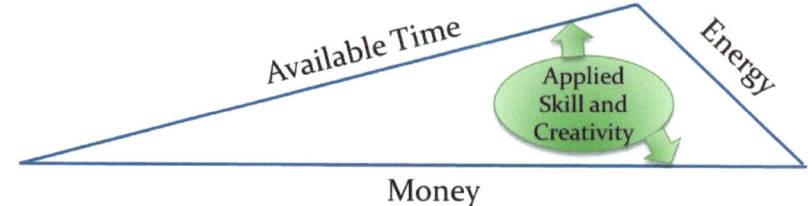

You can use your time and money, and apply some of your creative thinking and skills to come up with ways to use your time and money to boost your energy levels. Maybe you can do a good course in motivation or go on a refreshing vacation, or buy a case of energy drinks. (OK, that last one is seriously bad advice – but it is an option, right? A bad option. But an option. Don't make bad choices – even if you see them written in print as options.)

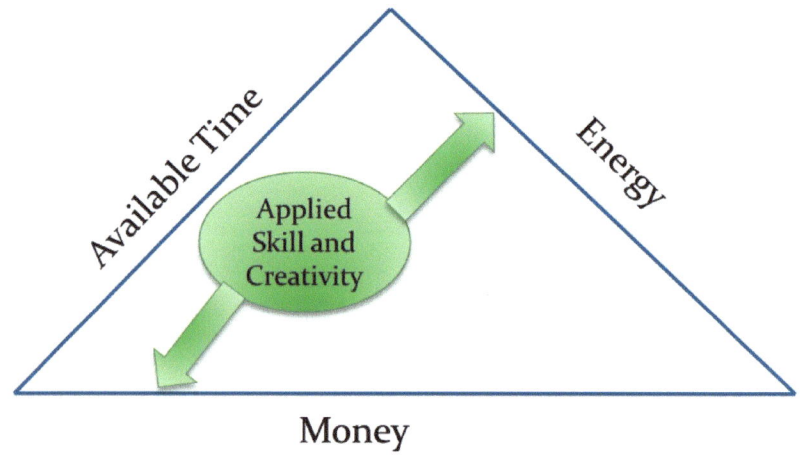

Similarly, if you lack money, but you have time available, and you are full of energy and vigor:

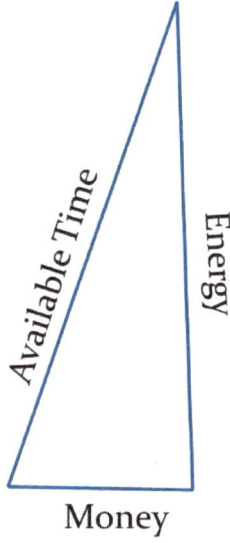

Money

You can apply your creativity and skills to your time and energy, and begin to deliver some service to society that is valuable, and for which you can get paid. Or you can use your energy and time to study something that can help you get promotion in your career so that you can earn more money.

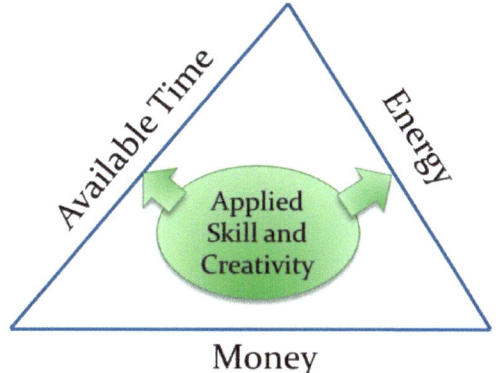

Money

One of the things about resources that we must always remember is that they reduce when used. If you have a pile of money, and you use some of that money, then the pile becomes smaller. If you are feeling all energetic now, so you decide to work through the night, three nights in a row, there will come a time when you will have used up all that energy. If you have nothing to do for the rest of the week, and you start making commitments to do things, then before you know it, all the available time in your week will be gone.

Skill and Creativity are not resources – so they are not subject to this restriction of scarcity. In fact, they work the opposite way. The more you use them, the better you become at them – so effectively the more you use them, the more of them you have.

Some of the most important skills you can acquire in life relate specifically to these three resources. Learning how to manage money effectively can enable you to achieve much more with the same amount. Learning to work efficiently and effectively can help you achieve more in the same amount of time. And taking some time to get to know your own emotions, and to learn how to manage them effectively so that they can serve you, rather than control you, can enable you to remain highly energetic through some of the toughest circumstances.

You will find that you live your best life when you have the Three Primary Resources in Balance

# Only By Going Smaller can you Grow Bigger

There is a very important balance, a dilemma as it were, which you need to be watching for. If you want to systematically grow your life, then watching this balance and continually working on it, is just about one of the most important things you can do.

The dilemma lies in this:

In order to grow your triangle, we've seen that you need Creativity and Skill. But generally, it costs time, money, and energy, to develop these faculties. Yes, some of them you can pick up "on the fly," e.g. during in-service training, and through experience. But in today's fast changing society, chances are that if you are not investing time, energy, and money into actively and deliberately building your skill set, learning to be more creative, and how to put that creativity into practical use, you will find your triangle either stagnating, or slowly beginning to shrink.

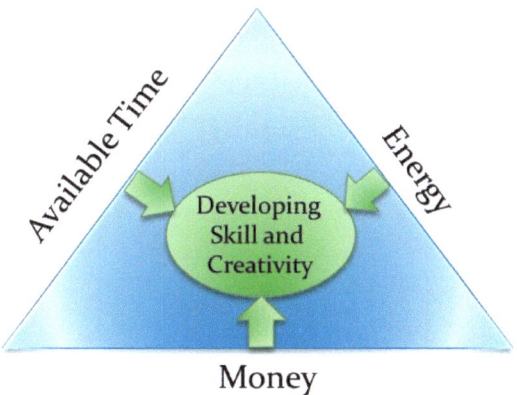

So the dilemma is that the moment you start spending time, energy and money on personal development activities, then your triangle immediately begins to shrink. However, the positive side is that as soon as these activities begin to bear fruit and give you practically useful skills and improved creative ability and processes, you will be able to grow your triangle back to what it was, and beyond that.

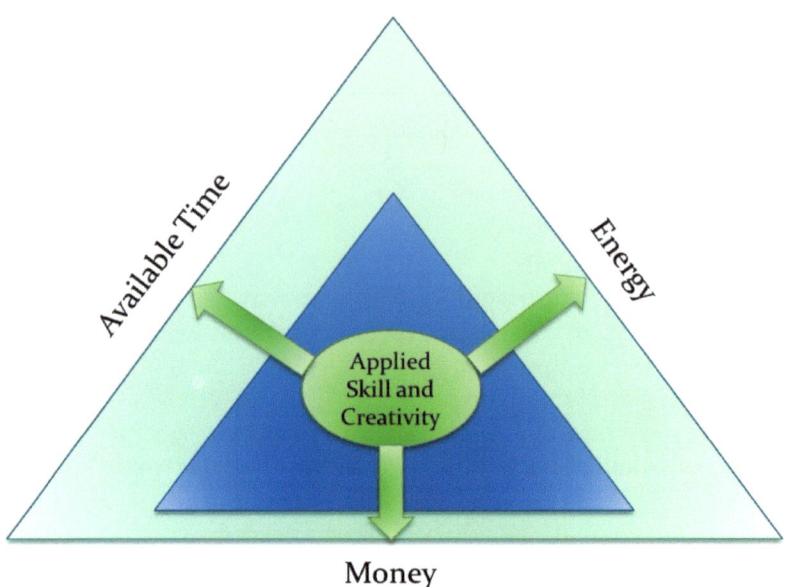

**Money**

The balance is that you must not spend so much time, energy, and money on self-development that your triangle collapses before you are able to begin to use what you are learning, to grow your triangle again.

# The Bad Luck of Good Luck

When you look at the statistics of people who have won large amounts of money, it is quite disturbing to see how many of them return to their former financial state, and even more surprising is how quickly this happens in many cases.

Similarly, it is interesting to see how many wealthy people get hit by a stroke of bad luck, lose most of what they have built up, and then a decade later are as wealthy as before, or more so.

What is this all about?

I will not claim that I have researched this to the point of trying to make a scientific statement here, but I have observed it enough to have formed at least a hypothesis on the matter, and my hypothesis is this:

The size and shape of our triangle will over time always settle back to reflect our ability to manage these three resources effectively – and that ability lies locked up in the skill set of our skill and creativity.

That means that if you suddenly won the lottery, or even had an unusual bit of luck in your business that caused it to grow massively in a very short time without much of your own doing, then you might for a period of time experience your triangle being huge, but it will most probably go back to the size that reflects what you are able to effectively manage, using your level of skills and creativity.

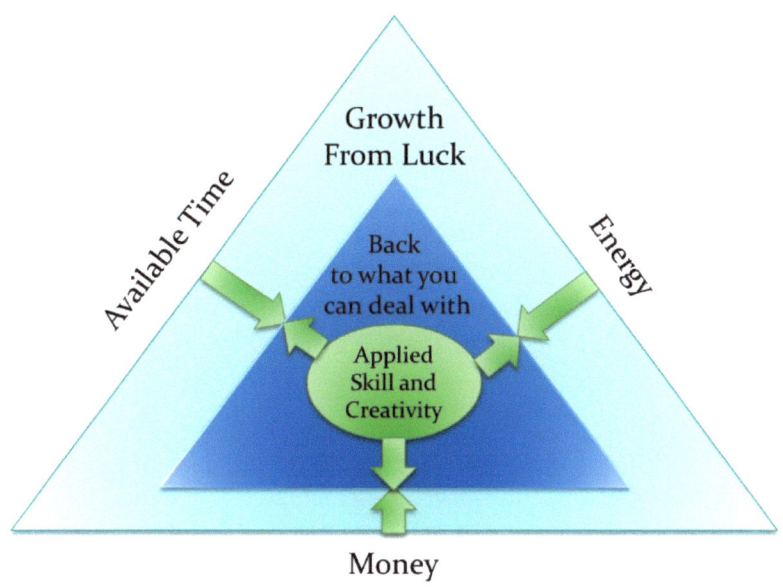

The bad luck of this is that often when people have gone through this, they have missed out on the process of systematically building skills that would have enabled them to utilise these sudden resources effectively. But the loss leaves them depressed – so that they would have actually been better off had they never had this stroke of luck.

So if you ever get lucky enough to find a sudden increase in your life brought about by none, or very little of your own doing, you would be wise to immediately move the money out of your reach – e.g. invest it for a year in a fixed deposit. Then begin to build your toolset. Read about financial management, get advice, and maybe even enrol in some structured study. William Cowie, Alex Green, and Warren Buffet are three people whose advice on investment should form part of the foundation of your money management skills.

In the same way, if you have developed your skills and creativity to a certain point, and a specifically strong piece of bad luck wiped out all or most of what you have achieved until now, in life, then you will find that over time, you can rebuild again what you had built before, using what you have available and systematically growing it by applying your skills and creativity.

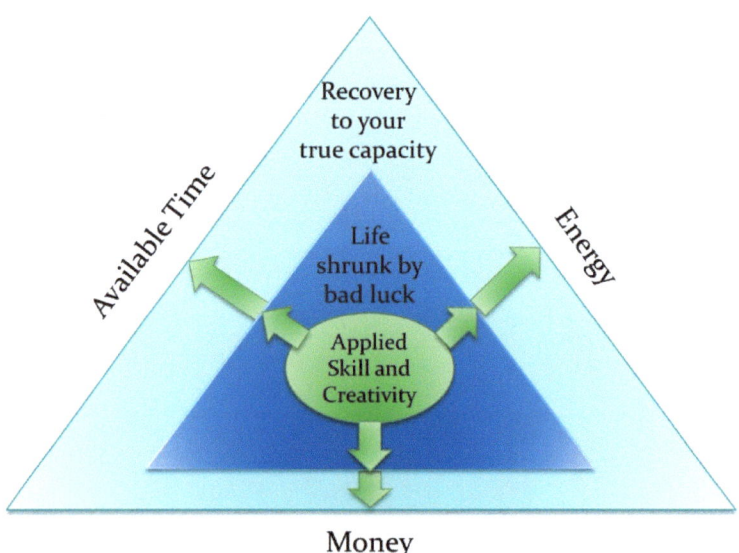

So if you suddenly find your life shrinking because of some bad luck, or a series of bad luck, don't lose hope. Realize that it is temporary, and that the life you have right now, is not really your life. It's a temporary set-back and you will get your life back.

Always remember, no matter what luck has done to you in your life – whether it threw you a false hope in the form of a large fortune which you have lost again, or whether it threw you a series of devastating blows that have left you gasping for emotional breath – whatever your current situation, by applying your skill and creativity, you can systematically begin to move your life forward again, and grow it, every day.

# The Definition of a Crisis

There is really only one crisis in life.

It is when you have run out of two of these at the same time.

If you have money, but no available time or energy, then you will just be miserably rich and busy.

If you have time, but you are depressed, and you have no money, you will not be able to motivate yourself to use your time usefully, and you won't have any money to try and get someone else to do anything useful on your behalf.

If you have energy, but you are so busy working on someone else's dreams, that you don't have a moment to spare, and you have no money of your own, you are stuck.

These are crises.

And we should avoid getting into any one of the above situations at all costs.

But as you could probably see from all the above examples, it is very, very seldom that we in modern society really get to a point where we have NONE of two or three of these resources.

Most of the time when you think you have "no time," you can find some time, somewhere, somehow, during which you can begin to do something.

Most of the time when you think you have "no money," you will find that you do still have some access to some money, somewhere, in one way or another.

Most of the time when you really feel that you have reached the end of your energy, you can actually still keep going for some time, or you can still find something to do that can be valuable, and that will reignite your interest and passion.

The good news then is that most of the time, if you look carefully, you will find that you have at least some, even if very little, of at least two of these resources. And if you have two, you can use those, together with your skills and ability, to build the third, and then begin to slowly and systematically build on all three.

Start where you are.

# Becoming Miserably Successful

A trap that many people fall into, is to decide that one of these three things is what is most important, and to become so focused on this one area, that the other areas suffer.

What happens when you have an extreme focus on one of the three resources, and you develop that with no effort at building the other two, is that one area of your life grows, whilst the other two remain stagnant, or even shrink. The result is a life that remains "small" in terms of real impact and especially in terms of personal fulfilment.

One of the most common traps is to focus on making lots of money. If you have lots of money, but no time to spend it or energy to enjoy using it in ways that are meaningful to you, then life is not great:

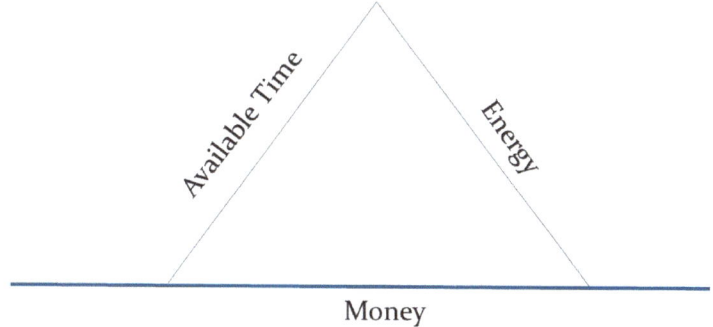

Money

If you have lots of time, but no energy – you are feeling depressed most of the time, and no money, then you will simply be bored. And although I have often wished for the luxury of sometimes being able to be bored, whenever I actually attained this, I discovered that boredom does not equate to a fulfilling life, it does not even equate to effective resting.

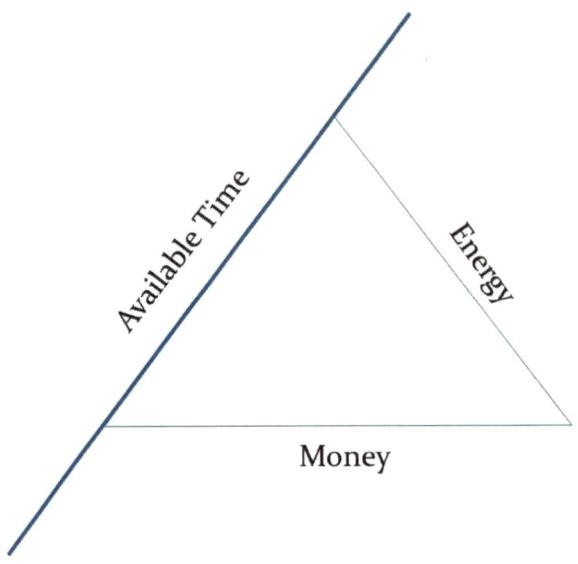

You live your best life when you hold your Three Primary Resources in balance.

# The Cost of Fickleness

Whenever you make a decision, the implementation of that decision would normally require at the very least the expenditure of time and energy, and in many cases also money.

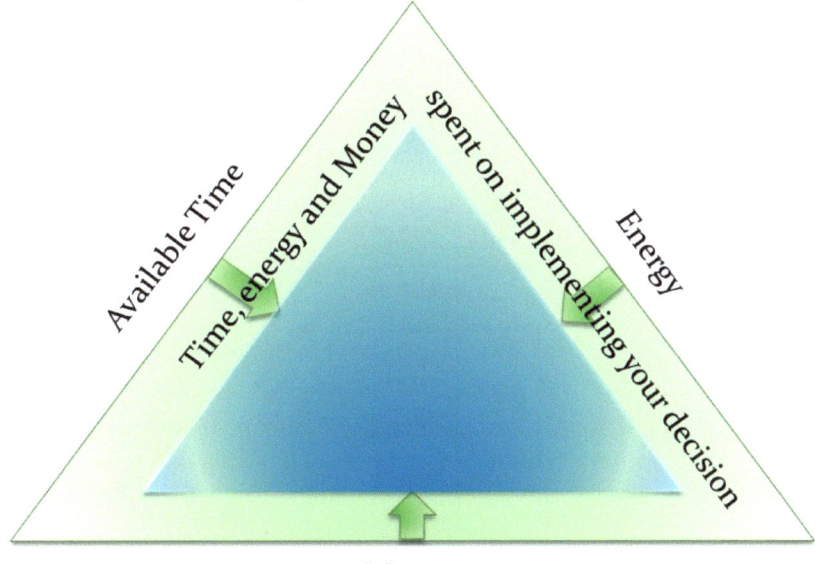

This means that every time you make a decision, and you start taking action towards that decision, the triangle of your life will shrink. The decision may be aimed at making the triangle grow, and it might do so after some time, but the immediate impact of beginning to implement a decision, is the shrinking of your triangle. There is a time lag between the beginning of implementing your decision, and your triangle beginning to grow again.

If you persist through this period, continuing to build your skills and creativity related to the way your decision is changing your environment, then after some time, the surface of your triangle will once again begin to expand, and it hopefully eventually will become even bigger than it was before.

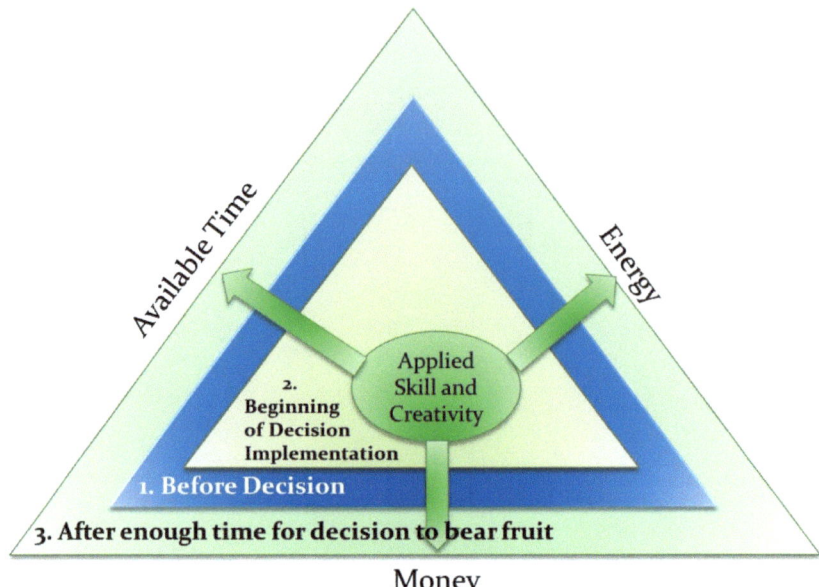

But if you are fickle, and keep changing your decision before you can see growth from your decision, you will at best slow down your growth significantly, or at worst, keep shrinking your triangle until you hit some major crisis in your life.

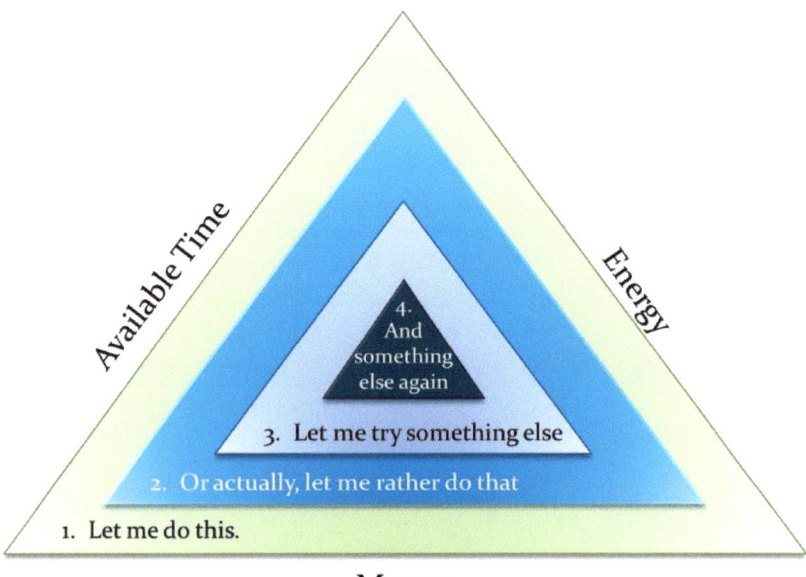

The best decisions in life are often not actually the best decisions in themselves, but they are the decisions that people have MADE the best by MAKING them work, through persistence and determination, and by constantly developing their skill and creativity in that area.

Decide what you want to do.

And do it.

One of the main reasons why people keep changing their decisions is because they fear that they've made the wrong decision. But when you persist in any area, you increase your skills, and you grow your creativity in that area. Your chances of success become greater every day. The one WRONG decision you can make in life, is to steer your life down a path of doing something you hate. Then you will learn to become better and better at the things you hate doing, and become more and more miserable as you become more and more successful, until one day, you suddenly burn out, and find yourself with no energy, all your time committed to something you hate, and probably also with little money, as you will have spent lots of money on buying stuff and doing things that could help you forget how much you hate your life.

As long as the things you are passionate about are part of your goals, and the things you love doing are part of what you decide to do, and you can see how your plan can help you over time keep your triangle in balance, you have a good chance that you're making good decisions, and if at first things seem a bit tough, you probably need persistence, more than a change of decision.

Of course there is a balance here. There is a limit to how far you should keep on banging your head against a wall in the hope of breaking through. But most people's problem is not that they persist too long, but that they change too often, because they haven't taken the time and effort to think about what they really wanted to do in the first place.

This book is not about decision making. But if you are not clear about what your passion is in life, about what really drives you, about what you enjoy doing, and about what you want to achieve in life, then I strongly suggest that you find some reading in those areas, and build those skills. Learn and practice to be creative in those areas, and then make a decision that you know you can be committed to. In my previous book *"When you lose yourself ... do you know where to go looking for you?"* I cover the topic of aligning your design, purpose and goals, in more depth.

# The Cost of Doing Too Many Things

There is a subtle form of trying to avoid decision making, called over-commitment. This happens when you are afraid of making the wrong decisions, so you don't actually make any decisions, you just try everything you can, and hope that something works, or even worse, to "see which one will work."

Trying to focus on too many things at the same time, fragments your life into multiple triangles. Each triangle can only have a small slice of your total available time, energy and money.

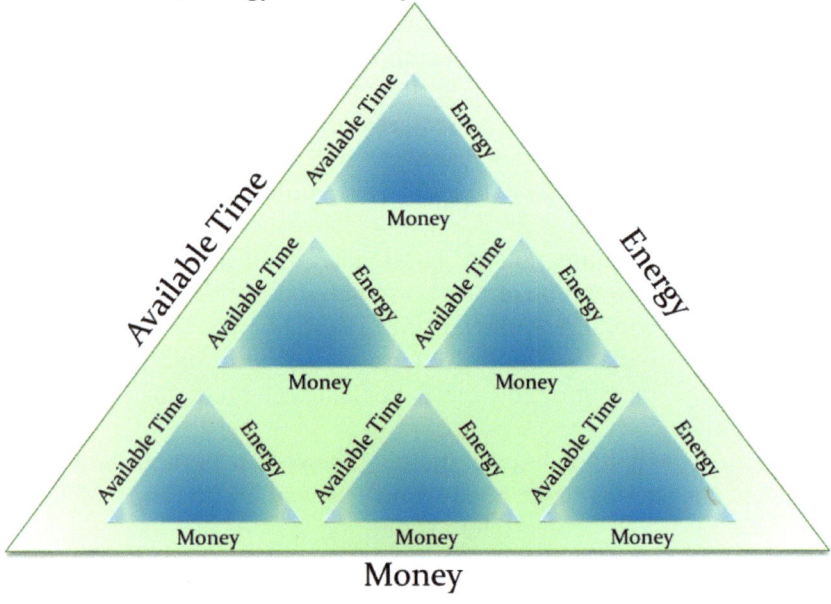

Most of us, when asked "What do you want to do?" either cannot come up with a clear answer, or we come up with a list of twenty things.

If you cannot make up your mind as to which of those things is most important to you, you will always be fragmenting your limited resources amongst a myriad of activities.

And you will have to spend time, energy, and possibly money, in building skills and creativity relating to each one of those things. What are the chances that you will actually ever reach a point of excellence in all of them? If you are like most normal human beings, you will just end up being mediocre at many things, and having little impact anywhere. And this despite the fact that you will be using every last minute of your time, spending every last ounce of your energy, and possibly also spending all your available money.

The word "decision" is made of two parts:

"de" - which generally means to take something away (think of words like dethrone, destabilise, decapitate).

"cision" which means to cut.

To make a decision, literally is to cut something away. It is to cut away everything that does not support the direction in which you want your life to go. It is to cut away that which hinders you and entangles your resources.

Remember, your resources are limited.

Use them for doing the things that really matter to you.

Focus on what matters. Make what you focus on, matter.

# The Power of Many

Obviously each human being has only 24 hours, of which a portion is already committed to sleeping, eating, going to the toilet and other non-negotiable activities, and for most of us a good portion of the remainder is also already committed to activities that have a varying level of impact on our ability to live the kind of lives we really want to have.

Similarly, none of us has limitless energy, and we tend to get tired, disillusioned, disappointed, worn out and suffer from many other emotional drains that can cause us to run out of energy.

We are all restrained by the law of scarcity, when it comes to our Three Primary Resources.

Herein lays the power of leadership and coordination. By learning how to effectively lead and coordinate the efforts of people, you can begin to use not only your own time, money and energy, but those of others, to help people together achieve joint goals and purposes.

This book is not about leadership. But if you want to live a life of impact beyond the size of your own personal triangle, learn the skills of leadership. Learn how to guide not only your own, but the creative processes of the people in the team or organisation that you choose to lead. One of the most valuable things any person can do for his community is to help people coordinate their efforts to achieve more than any one of them would have been able to do alone. For more about the fundamentals of leadership, I have written the book "Developing the Heart of a Leader."

Learn to do this, and you will find that people will willingly make their resources available to you.

# Your Organisation or Team

If you are already in a leadership position, however senior or junior, it means that you are responsible for the impact that your organisation or team will have on its world.

It doesn't matter how you define that impact – whether it's about internal service delivery if you are a service or project team, or about customer service if you are a customer facing team, or if it's about shareholder value or social impact. Whatever you have defined as your important goals: That is the impact that you want to make.

Your team has the same three primary resources. You all have a certain amount of time available – your working time (and some more if you work after hours). You all have limited energy, and the way you treat each other and work together has a very significant impact on the amount of that energy. You have a certain amount of money to work with.

Your team has skills and creativity. It is your task as leader to coordinate those skills, and harness that creativity, in order to achieve the best possible results for your team.

By keeping the philosophy of the three triangles in mind, you can have a simple subjective measuring stick to help you be aware of where you are strong and weak, and to help you take action.

This book is not about organisational leadership, or team management. But if you are in a position where you are responsible for a team of people, then make sure that you develop the skills needed to manage money effectively in an organisational context. Make sure you know what your budgets mean, make sure you are thinking about what the outlook in your markets are and what that means for your team. Make sure you are watching the money-side of your team's triangle.

You also need to be a source of energy and of coaching your people through helping them build more energy. You need to know about emotional intelligence, how to motivate people, how to not burn them out, and how to not allow your team to go into group-induced slacking. Read about these things. Learn about them. Your skills and creativity in this area can help you continually build and strengthen the energy side of your team's triangle. Marcus Buckingham probably understands more about this than most people. Read his books.

You need to know about managing your own time, and assigning your people's time efficiently and effectively to accomplish the most important tasks in the least possible time with the machinery, infrastructure and resources to your avail. You are responsible to make sure that your team delivers to its maximum potential in the time that is available, and that it does not waste the time that you are being paid for them to deliver. For that, knowing about Theory of Constraints is possibly one of the most important foundations you can lay. Buy the book "The Goal," then "It's not Luck" and then the "Theory of Constraints Handbook."

And of course, if you want your team to be systematically expanding its triangle, you need to be continually developing your team's skills and creativity, and especially its ability to operate together as an effective team.

# The Power of One

This section might seem as if I am in a way repeating what I've already said, but it's important enough to be said very specifically and clearly, in case you did not get it the first time, or the second time.

You will live your most effective life when you can identify the one most important thing that you want to do with your life, and begin to focus all your available time, all your energy, and all the money you can spare, towards accomplishing that goal.

Most people cannot immediately drop everything they are doing, and suddenly start doing their ONE thing.

But that is actually not most people's biggest problem. Most people's biggest problem is that when you ask them, "What do you WANT to do?" they cannot give you a clear answer of the ONE thing that they want to do, more than anything else.

The moment you can answer that question, you can begin to make decisions that begin to move your life in that direction.

And when you start making decisions, continually consider your triangle.

If you are planning to quit your job to pursue your passion and doing work you love, spend some time to calculate how long it will take before your passion will start earning you money. And then make sure that the money-leg of your triangle won't run out before then. If it seems that it will, plan more carefully, work a bit longer in that dead-end job and save every penny. Use every bit of your free time to learn about your passion, rather than to just go out and have fun. That way you will probably spend less money – which means you can save faster, and you will begin to generate more and more passion – building up energy.

If you know that pursuing your passion requires a lot of time, then think carefully before trying to begin to pursue it part-time, because then you will soon collapse the time-side of your triangle, and to compensate for that, you will sleep less and less, until you run out of energy. Maybe you should think harder about how to make it a sustainable business, get some investors, and start full-time with a big bang.

I'm not saying don't pursue your passion. On the contrary, it's the most important thing you can do in life. But as you prepare to do that, keep your Three Primary Resources in mind, and make sure that you've thought about the impact that every decision you make, is going to have on them. If you think your triangle cannot handle a major career shift, try to break it into a series of smaller shifts that gradually move you in the right direction, without collapsing your triangle – even better if you can continually slowly keep growing it whilst moving in the direction of your passion.

One of the best collections of resources around this is the Live Your Legend community run by Scott Dinsmore.

You will find that your energy-side of the triangle tends to naturally grow stronger and stronger as you move closer to your passion. In fact, often when you feel you have no energy left for a job you hate, you can go home and work another eight hours straight, doing something you really love.

So figure out ONE thing: What do you WANT to do.

Do that thing first.

If you really have time, energy and money left after that, then by all means start doing the second thing, and the third.

But first do ONE well.

That is how you will grow your triangle.

That is how you will live a life of impact.

What do you want to do?

# About the Author

It has taken me a long time to figure out what I really am interested and passionate about. After school I did some mission work, then did compulsory service in the defence force for two years, and thereafter found a job as an office cleaner in a cardboard factory. From there I went into the insurance industry where I was reasonably successful and desperately unhappy. Quitting in sheer desperation, I tried to start a business, failed miserably, and after several months of living on bread and potatoes, went back into insurance. I got a good pay-back from tax because of the period that I was without income, and used that to pay for the studies an exams to become a Microsoft Certified Systems Engineer. For a few years I was very happy working in the IT industry, became manager, and later national operations manager. I worked 7 days a week, 16 hours a day, leading the department to pretty astounding results, while also leading a youth group on the side for one of the largest churches in our city – and then promptly burnt out. I took a break, went to China, spent a year rediscovering myself, went back to "normal" work, began to do some management consulting and became strategic manager and later director of a non-profit organisation. From here I started lecturing at a business school part time, and later at an university. I found some opportunities consulting more in the international market – which brought me to where I am today, as change management coordinator for the China plant of an international off-shore company.

During all this time, I continually studied, and completed first a Bachelors in Management and then a Masters in Managing and Leading Innovation and Change.

I am fascinated by, and therefore incessantly read and write about the integration of design, purpose and calling with performance and success as a foundation for living a successful, fulfilling and meaningful life; and about the way this scales into the design, purpose, performance and success of teams, organisations, and societies.

Ashton Fourie
22 May 2015
Xiamen, China
ashton@ashtonfourie.com